The ElderGarten

A Field Guide
for the Journey of a Lifetime

By Sally Z. Hare

The ElderGarten
Copyright © 2023
still learning, inc

ISBN: 978-0-9895042-9-4

Comments or questions:
Dr. Sally Z. Hare, couragetoteach@sc.rr.com

Cover art by Jane Zalkin who, after a long life of teaching kindergarten, followed the Beauty she loved into becoming an artist.
Jane lives in Mt. Pleasant, SC.

Book design by Jim R. Rogers

Prose Press
Pawleys Island, SC
prosencons@live.com

Dedication

To my teachers, Jim and Ben
and Parker and Elaine
and my sisters, Susan and Jane,
and Aunt B
And the Ancestors, Ida and Miss Mason
And all the Dogs I have ever loved

Contents

Intermezzo
After Reading Alice Walker's
There Is a Flower at the End of My Nose Smelling Me

27

Mystery: My Story

Steppingstone to Portal

The Beauty I Love

Intermezzo
Stepping stones

38

Beauty as a Steppingstone

Seed Corn

The Day the Rain Came

Of Grief and Play and Creativity

Intermezzo
A Woman's Garden of Verse

Preface
A Note to Readers from the Author and her Writing Group

Dear Reader,

Welcome to this field guide to the journey of a lifetime.

I welcome your joining my quest to connect soul and role as Elder by seeking what Thomas Merton called our hidden wholeness. In creating the space for that, I name and claim what matters, beginning by reclaiming words that our culture may demean or misuse.

I love the idea that the root word of *glossary* is *gloss*, so the glossary (near the end of the field guide) offers you a collection of textual glosses. I hope these words shine as I take back what matters by naming what the words mean in this context. You may even want to begin in the glossary!

Writing is a paradox: it is both individual work – and it takes a community. My community started as a temporary writing support group on Zoom more than a year ago. The Courage to Write has become a source of truth and deep listening every Monday, a portal into a new week. As the members listened *The ElderGarten* into being, one person spoke: "You need a preface that will speak to Readers and offer them a reason to trust what you are telling them."

They share their reasons with you – and I share my gratitude for them – and for you.

With hope and respect and gratitude,

Sally Z. Hare

Veta Goler, Retreat facilitator, artist, and retired Spelman College professor

As a long-time meditator and self-described mystic, I value inner work deeply. In my view, the complex societal and world problems we face today can only be resolved through ways of being and doing that arise out of sustained inner work. By exploring who we are as individual human beings, we come to know our connection to each other and every other thing on the planet. And the love for ourselves that we develop through self-knowledge is essential for us to love others. We turn inward in whatever ways work for us to develop and access love for ourselves, which we then offer to others, to the world. In short, inner work helps us know how to be so we can know what to do.

Sally Z. Hare knows this. She has lived this for most of her years on the planet. And through her teaching, retreats, mentorships, and friendships, she has shared with others this knowledge, as well as practices, ways of thinking, and exploration opportunities that help others to do inner work effectively. The ElderGarten: A Field Guide for the Journey of a Lifetime is another step Sally is taking to help us know the importance of inner work and how we might approach it for our own good and for the good of the world.

Sally's message is especially helpful for those of us who may feel that we no longer have much to offer the world because of our age, because we are older. She makes it clear that we have much to offer! But her message is not just for older people. Through this beautiful text, we learn that to best offer our gifts to the world as elders, we must begin learning how to do so earlier in life. In this way, The ElderGarten is for younger people, as well.

*If you are reading this book, you are probably already
contemplating how best to share your gifts with the world.
In this text you will find profound ways of knowing, being,
and doing that Sally has developed through her lived
experience — and ongoing reading and research! — and
how to apply them to your own life. You will discover how
living and loving yourself fully will connect you to others
and contribute to a movement that is saving the world.*

***

Jean M. Richardson, Co-Founder of Courageous
Commons; progressive pastor and activist in the
Presbyterian Church USA; former Executive Director
of Kirkridge Retreat and Study Center

*Long before I met Dr. Sally Z. Hare, she and her partner
Jim R. Rogers created still learning, inc., dedicated to the
quest of lifelong learning for all adults. This commitment to
lifelong learning, her love of research and reading stacks of
books has never ceased in Sally's life, which turns out to be
a gift for all of us.*

*In my own life, I have come to experience Sally as the
quintessential educator whose gifts always create a
trustworthy space. She has enabled me to see my own
deep potential. For years I have experienced her insightful
leadership as an invitation into my own journey, calling
me to pull from the roots of my own courage and lay claim
to my own hidden gifts.*

*Becoming an elder has no age requirement, so no matter
the decade of your life, I invite you now to say "yes" to
Sally's ElderGarten. This book speaks clearly to her deep*

lifelong value of "still learning" as she plants for us the seeds she believes are needed to create an ElderGarten in your own life. Opening this book promises to inspire you to weed, till and cultivate new seeds in your life.

Reader, beware: you may be changed as you open these pages and take your own journey toward becoming an Elder.

***

Haqiqa Bolling, Educator, Activist, Convener of Circles

If you are reading this preface then you have already decided to give this book a try, or you are at least considering it. Perhaps you already know author Sally Z. Hare, in which case you have no need of more assurances of her deep and rich gifts that you will find infused in these pages. Or perhaps you have picked this up because the idea of *The ElderGarten* is speaking to you. Either way, as you turn the pages of this book, you will quickly know you are in good hands.

When I put my trust in someone, it is generally because they have shown themselves over time to be worthy of it. Sally has been practicing the art of living an authentic life the 30+ years I have known her. You will find in reading the stories of her life that are embedded in this book, and from which she draws life lessons, she has been living authentically for far longer. Sally doesn't pretend to be an expert, but rather a companion on the journey. She offers a road map, or rather a "field guide" to a way of living with curiosity; deeply listening within as well as to the world around us; drawing out the threads of life's lessons and meaning-making in the hopes of living intentionally, authentically, and full-heartedly.

May it be so!

* * *

Jonetta Moyo, founder of My Inspiration Studio, a curated space to journal and create connections with yourself and others

The ElderGarten is Dr. Sally Z. Hare's birdsong. It is an eloquent and melodic offering from her beautifully crafted "nest" of wholeness, hope and love. With her song she beckons us to become more aware of the importance of our presence in this world and to journey into greater depth of who we are. In her field guide, Sally profoundly shares that she has "embraced her role as Elder and courageously being present in this transitory life." This courage is simply who Sally is. Her courageousness has uplifted and inspired me on my own journey. Over the last decade, I have been fortunate to have Sally's song as an accompaniment through various transitions in my life. She has welcomed me to explore elderhood in community and on my own. On this journey, I have discovered a greater understanding of what it means to courageously be myself and to take my gifts, my wisdom and the beauty that I am into every space and place that I occupy. With Sally's offering of *The ElderGarten*, you will feel welcomed and invited and encouraged to see your gifts, to embrace your wholeness and renew your understanding of what it

v

means to be you. Allow Sally to introduce you to the role of Elder and you will gain an awareness of why sharing the Beauty you love is sacred and necessary.

***

Caroline Fairless, author of *The God Presumption, The Space Between Church & Not-Church ~ A Sacramental Vision for the Healing of Our Planet,* and *The Dance of the Caterpillars ~ In a Time Before Texting.* A Courage facilitator, Caroline was ordained in the Episcopal Church in 1989.

Unlike a GPS map that directs you from starting point to destination along the fastest route possible, Sally Z. Hare's Field Guide for The Journey of a Lifetime *removes concepts of linear, fast, and end point. Push a little harder about where you begin to step into this journey toward becoming an Elder: she will tell you, "Wherever you are at the moment." Again, unlike a GPS map, this process doesn't seek to avoid obstacles, but to engage and navigate them.*

The ElderGarten *is about integrity, both personal and communal. It is about becoming whole in the sense of bringing your inner and outer worlds together, into a unique way of being. It's about identifying and growing your particular gifts – Sally names them birthright gifts – that emerge from learning what you love, what gives you joy.*

The ElderGarten *speaks to the recognition of your life patterns – the ever-changing fluidity of hope and possibility – and asks of you the question, "How can I direct my passions and talents for the enrichment of the earth community?" Sally's work transcends the paradox of community and selfhood and calls us to a vision of what is emerging. And so this book is also about formation – not into a particular way of being – but according to who you are and how you might imagine your birthright gifts in service to the whole. I look at this process of becoming an Elder as a canvas whose colors never dry. Always a new color, a new shape, a new pattern, and all that wisdom passed along. The great privilege offered to all of us in this field guide to* The ElderGarten *is to leave the last brush stroke wet.*

The ElderGarten:

A Field Guide for the Journey of a

Lifetime

My mother often told the story that I ran away from home to go to kindergarten. My version was a bit different: I had been waiting my whole life for my fifth birthday. Five-year-olds were supposed to go to kindergarten, but my mother had decided not to send me. She worried I might feel pushed out of the nest as our family of four added the newest baby girl.

So I took matters into my own hands.

The day after my birthday I awakened early, quietly dressed and headed downstairs to the apartment of my best friend, Irwin. Irwin was three months older, so I made complete sense of the fact that he already attended kindergarten and would be the perfect partner for my first day.

"I am going to kindergarten with you today," I informed Irwin. His mother (I called her Aunt Sara out of respect) assumed my mother had approved; her hug left me wrapped in the scent of wintergreen.

Unselfconsciously holding hands with Irwin as we walked around the corner to the school, I stopped to pick up several perfect leaves on the Charleston sidewalk: a red maple, a brown-with-yellow-specks oak, a gold gingko. I offered them as a gift to my new teacher, oblivious to her calling my mother (everyone knew everyone in this neighborhood) and convincing her to let me stay.

Mother and I told different stories, but they resulted in the same happy ending: I was a kindergarten student. That happy ending was also the happy beginning on a path that would set the direction for my life. I felt at home in this space that invited me to be my best self with everything I needed: community, stories, music, play, snacks, quiet time, naps, and sympathy for my falls with encouragement to try again. We laughed and cried; we cleaned up our messes; we admired each other's gifts and began to glimpse our own.

From Kindergarten to ElderGarten

Now I yearn for a space like the kindergarten I once knew: a space of play and joy; space for learning and opportunities for continued growth that is inner and outer. I name what I need as the ElderGarten, the space for me to grow into becoming an Elder.

Elder is the time of Life when meaning blooms from a lifetime of seeds. An Elder lives with authenticity, with integrity. *Integrity*, from the Latin *integer* meaning whole or complete, feels like the right word to describe what I know is my work now: connecting my Inner Self, my soul, with how I show up in my outer world, my role. That word *integrity* resonates with my knowing that Elder is not synonymous with old person, though becoming an Elder is certainly the journey of a lifetime.

The words of the poetic Elder, Wendell Berry, ring true:

> And the world cannot be discovered by a journey of miles, no matter how long, but only by a spiritual journey, a journey of one inch, very arduous and humbling and joyful, by which we arrive at the ground at our own feet and learn to be at home.
>
> -- Wendell Berry, *The Unforeseen Wilderness: Kentucky's Red River Gorge*

Learning to be at home resounds deeply with uniting soul and role as Elder: home as True Self, home as knowing the ground on which we stand. This non-linear journey of a lifetime begins early in life. Unlike the kindergarten of my younger life, the ElderGarten won't fit neatly into a classroom or an academic year. Instead, I envision the field described by the Sufi poet Rumi:

> **Out beyond ideas of wrongdoing and rightdoing, there is a field. I'll meet you there.**
>
> **When the soul lies down in that grass, the world is too full to talk about. Ideas, language, even the phrase *each other* doesn't make any sense.**
>
> **-- *The Essential Rumi*, translated by**
>
> **Coleman Barks**

I know that field holds my best chance of meeting my Self as Elder, of living into that role. To find this ElderGarten, this field for learning to be an Elder, I turn to my most important teachers: words and reading and writing.

My Need for a Field Guide

Books are the thin places (in Celtic spirituality, thin places are where heaven and earth seem to touch; please see glossary near the end of the book for words that pique your interest) that invite me into the space between the real and the imaginal, so why not a field guide that shows the way to the ElderGarten? My Reader Self immediately goes to the library to find the right book. I can't locate the field guide I need in the library or the bookstore or even on the internet, so I decide to write it.

My Reader Self writes so I can read my own words, hear my own thinking. As I begin to do that, I see with fresh eyes this field of wholeness, of connectedness, where even the phrase each other doesn't make any sense. I have glimpsed that field again and again in my lifetime, and yet finding it eludes me.

That field is and has always been within reach, but my map is outdated and inadequate for finding the place I seek. Perhaps writing a field guide will show me the way.

First Glance at Mortality

A few months after becoming a kindergartener, I was awakened earlier than usual by a strange sound. I slowly sat up, trying to make sense of the guttural moans. A light from the kitchen illuminated the familiar figure of Daddy, sitting on my bed in the early morning darkness. My heart raced as I tentatively touched his arm.

Tears were streaming down his face, his breath ragged gulps. I had never seen my father cry.

"Daddy?" I whispered tentatively, torn between embracing him and hiding under the sheets.

"Grandma died," he managed to gasp. Still unsure of whether to be afraid or astounded, I inched closer, putting my arms around him.

As I tried to comfort my father and make sense of his

tears, I vaguely grasped that Grandma was my father's mother, but not that my father was her child: he was a grownup. Do grownups cry? Children cry when their pets die, but people don't die; do they? How can mothers die? I couldn't have articulated any of that complexity then. With this first glance at mortality, of the cycle of life, my chest tightened, and empathetic tears spilled from my eyes.

Now I understand that moment as a significant start on the path to Rumi's field where the world is too full to talk about. Becoming an Elder takes a lifetime, but our culture's obsession with youth makes it difficult to find the motivation to make the required commitment. Such a journey requires intention and attention; a commitment to nurturing the seeds of True Self with which we are born.

An Elder embodies living undivided, claiming a life in which the inner Self is integral with ways of being in the outer world, claiming one's story. With no small amount of trepidation, I know I must offer my story as the basis for this field guide. Frederick Buechner's words help me find the confidence to share my story, my journey:

> **Who cares if I tell my story or share my journey? What in the world could be less important than who I am and who my mother and father were, the mistakes I have made together with the occasional**

discoveries, the bad times and good times, the moments of grace....I talk about my life anyway because if, on the one hand, hardly anything could be less important, hardly anything could be more important. My story is important not because it is mine... but because if I tell it anything like right, the chances are you will recognize that in many ways it is also yours.

Maybe nothing is more important than that we keep track, you and I, of the stories of who we are and where we have come from and the people we have met along the way... (T)o lose track of our stories is to be profoundly impoverished not only humanly but also spiritually.

I not only have my secrets, I am my secrets. And you are yours. Our secrets are human secrets, and our trusting each other enough to share them with each other has much to do with the secret of what it means to be human.

--Frederick Buechner, *Telling Secrets*

My life is **not** my story; my story is the way I make sense of my life, how I tell it. We must be the authors of our own stories, claiming the authority for knowing what they mean, for constructing that meaning.

Becoming an Elder means acknowledging my power

to construct the meaning of my life. Yes, the journey is about meaning, but not about finding some universal meaning of life, as I once thought. No, it is about going back and remembering and claiming MY meaning, YOUR meaning.

We do that by discovering and uncovering steppingstones: the people and the places, the words and the music and the moments that we have encountered along the way. They are what the brain scientists tell us we store as individual and distinct moments, what they call event segmentation. I call them steppingstones – and I share this field guide in support of our traveling back to retrieve those moments, so we can examine them in the Light of Now and see what's there.

Only I can tell my own story – and yet I CANNOT tell my story anything like right without the help of a trustworthy community. So I invite you to join me in finding the courage to make sense of life – mine and yours.

Becoming an Elder is the journey of a lifetime, the way to wholeness – and I offer you *The ElderGarten* as the field manual. Reading my own words, I become even more aware that this journey is both inner and outer and that I need resilience to resist the urge to prematurely leave or let go, to rashly cling or hold on, or to collapse in exhaustion and despair.

Resilience is not a gene or a birthright gift; the root of resilience is the Latin *resilio*, to jump back. Resilience grows out of practices that allow us to jump back into our lives, our memories, our experiences, in order to live into the role of Elder and discern the meaning of life. I want to share those practices with you. The practices are not linear, so I won't give you a list. Instead I offer them as they emerge in my stories, so I ask you to let go of moving in a straight line and to read in circles. The best way I can explain is to offer you this wisdom from the Traveling Jewish Theatre in *Coming from a Great Distance:*

Stories move in circles. They don't go in straight lines. So it helps if you listen in circles. There are stories inside stories and stories between stories, and finding your way through them is as easy and as hard as finding your way home. And part of the finding is the getting lost. And when you're lost, you start to look around and to listen.

I offer you a poem and an empty page as a resting place between the circles, as an intermezzo. A breathing space. A place to hear your Self.

Intermezzo

A Short Course in Ubuntu

This being human

Is a Paradox.

I enter and leave

Alone

and yet

the Journey requires

companionship.

We are hardwired

To connect.

The very act of

Learning

is Social.

I am I

because You are You.

-- Sally Z. Hare

Notes to Me

I learned fear from my Mother. She taught me well. Dogs were a major object of our fear: my Little-Girl Self panicked when I spotted a dog. Heart racing, I crossed the street, going out of my way to avoid any kind of encounter with that four-legged creature.

At age ten, I stopped being afraid.

Learning and Unlearning

Sitting in Miss Behlmer's fifth grade class, second row, third desk, I awaited my turn to read aloud from our health book. One paragraph per person, up and down the rows (at times so slowly that my Reader Self cringed), we trudged through a chapter about a little girl's fear of dogs – and her father's gift of a puppy to help the child overcome her fear.

An insight landed hard and my whole body tensed with energy: fear was learned. That new understanding thrust its way from my head to my heart to my stomach and traveled all the way down to my toes. The awareness moved inside me: fear was learned; fear could be unlearned.

The sun was shining in the long antique windows, playing with Miss Behlmer's navy dress. (All her dresses were navy or black. Sometimes I would notice streaks of purple; sometimes, blue.) Tommy stuttered as he read his passage aloud, the way he always did. Freddy threw a spitball at Janice, the way he always did. Irwin's stomach growled, the way it always did. The faded blue textbook seemed to expand in my hands, feeling bigger and more significant.

Going back to the memory, I discover a steppingstone on my journey to becoming an Elder.

Elder is Not About Age

Aging is a privilege that begins with the moment of birth. If we are lucky, we continue to age every hour of every day. Life expectancy across the planet has increased rapidly since the early nineteenth century, although the inequality of how long we can expect to live is still massive within and across countries. In our pre-modern, poor world, the life span was around thirty years everywhere. Yet Elders were important in those early cultures – and oral and written history suggest that we have always had Elders.

We have more old people on the planet than ever before, but fewer Elders. And more than ever, we need Elders. Elder is not about age, but about committing with intention to the lifelong journey to wholeness and meaning-making.

The path is an individual one – **and** it is too hard to travel alone. Already paradoxes appear – and I realize one of my practices is learning to embrace *both/and* in a culture that is *either/or*. Already I see my Elder role as courageously being present in this transitory life, this thin time when the veil often feels paradoxically rigid and fragile between what is and what could be, between the material and the spiritual.

I understand in a new way the importance of grief as inner work in the face of loss in our outer world. I recognize griefwork as entering a thin place that offers us the opportunity for our hearts to break open.

> *There are at least two ways to picture a broken heart...*
>
> *The conventional image, of course, is that of a heart broken by unbearable tension into a thousand shards--shards that sometimes become shrapnel aimed at the source of our pain...*
>
> *Here, the broken heart is an unresolved wound that we too often inflict on others. But there is another way to visualize what a broken heart might mean. Imagine that small, clenched fist of a heart 'broken open' into largeness of life, into greater capacity to hold one's own and the world's pain and joy...*
>
> *Here heartbreak becomes a source of healing, enlarging our empathy and extending our ability to reach out.*
>
> -- Parker J. Palmer, *The Politics of the Broken-Hearted*

As I ponder practices, my friend Caroline suggests the metaphor of Sankofa, a mythical bird who walks forward as she looks backward. A symbol of the Akan people who today live primarily in Ghana and Ivory Coast in West Africa, the bird is carrying an egg in her mouth. She gives permission to go back and remember what we might have forgotten.

As I learn more about Sankofa, I realize the Akan ancestors understood that life can only be lived forward and understood backward long before Danish theologian Soren Kierkegaard wrote those words. I envision a sacred seed in the bird's beak, my seed of True Self instead of an egg, as she grants me permission (actually she gives me a nudge, a push) to go back and look at things I've saved, from letters to quotes, from my high school sweatshirt (Go Bantams!) to Aunt Gussie's tiny treasure chest from a shop in Paris. As we get better acquainted, the Sankofa bird often takes advantage of a song or a smell to take me back to a person or a place or a moment.

Living into Caroline's suggestion of Sankofa as my guide on this journey, I am aware of my apprehension about appropriating stories and traditions and rituals and beliefs that come from another culture. I find myself thinking about the difference in appropriating, that is, stealing or taking something that clearly is not mine, and honoring something because it resonates

15

with my heart. Instead of appropriation, I determine to find a respectful way of appreciating and learning from other cultures.

Already this Bird feels like more than my guide; I need her as my companion, as my teacher, as my inspiration, as my muse. I respectfully acknowledge the Akan Sankofa as she speaks to me across years and miles and cultural differences. Even now the Sankofa bird brings back smells and sounds and faces as I remember my time in West Africa a few years ago. I am quickly immersed once again in the sense of home that filled my heart when I walked on the Benin coast: the food, the music, the people felt familiar.

A memory returned of my scooping up a shell that looked like one on my South Carolina beach. The sand on this beach in Ouidah was the same color as the sand along the SC coast. The dunes were covered with similar grasses. The trees looked like the ones at home. The ocean waves broke and rolled ashore just as they did on my beloved coast.

I wondered how that must have seemed to the captured Africans some 200 to 300 years ago. I wondered, if after months of darkness in the holds of slave ships, their first glimpse of land on the Carolina coast felt familiar. I wondered if they experienced a wild and desperate hope that they had returned to Africa instead of landing in America, heading into a life of generational enslavement.

Once again I do not realize the importance of the moment, of another steppingstone, as I appreciate in a new way, from the inside out, that Southern culture is indeed born out of the convergence of African and European peoples. I know a sense of home, of discovering my ancestors, and I resonate with the local proverb, "*Se wo were fi na wosankofa a yenkyi*: It is not wrong to go back for that which you have forgotten."

I learn that Akan culture can also be found in the Americas, especially in the Southern United States where as many as ten percent of all slave ships that landed in South Carolina, where I now live, may have contained Akan people. As I connect soul and role as Elder, I want to discard my scarcity mindset that, as a second-generation well-assimilated white American, I have no ancestors. Rather I want to claim an abundance that embraces ALL my ancestors included in my rich Southern culture as well as in my Eastern European heritage. I embrace the etymology of this word from the Akan language (also known as *Twi/Fante*): *San* -- to return, *Ko* – to go, *Fa* – to fetch, to seek and take.

Living into Wholeness Requires Remembering

I left home when I was almost three.

My Mother often told me the story of my packing a tiny suitcase and moving in with my grandparents when my sister was born. Her voice held pride and chagrin as she recollected my insistence that I would return when the baby stopped crying.

That summer was an important steppingstone on my journey to becoming an Elder. Ida and Harry (I always called my grandparents by their first names at their request, even though I often received lectures about disrespect from other adults) and I worked together to prepare meals and to clean up: Ida washed and I dried and Harry put the tableware in the right drawer or cabinet. I remember Harry's encouraging me to find a spot of food on a dish and give it back to Ida for another washing; he always laughed when that happened. They could be serious and ever so silly.

We napped together and played together. I don't remember having a bedtime or meals that differed from theirs; I felt like I belonged. They read to me; I learned to embroider and play pinochle and gin rummy. I cherished the simple patterns of our days, of our time; nothing felt rushed. Anger and grief were as welcome as laughter and affection. I learned so much about what mattered. Then, in the intervening decades, I forgot my own knowing.

A few years ago, when I reached the age of 70, I spent time reflecting on how I would name my work now. I wanted to be purposeful about living into wholeness, about showing up fully for the rest of my life, about moving with integrity. What I quickly discovered was that 70 is very late to begin connecting soul and role as Elder. I had a sense of clarity that this was a journey, not a destination or a goal – and that waiting until 70 meant I had a lot of remedial work to do.

So I began the work of unlearning. I found it hard – and exhausting – and a bit depressing. I realized I would need practices to find the resilience to stay with the work.

As I began to pay attention, I realized those practices were already present in my life; that in fact, I had used some of them for many years. Now I wanted to be more deliberate in naming and living into the practices I deemed essential.

For many years, I had suggested the practice of noticing and naming and nurturing in my retreats and classes. As a teacher who has always valued creating space for others, I often gave permission to "just notice." I heard myself say that naming and nurturing can come later... right now it's fine to just notice.

So I gave myself permission to "just notice," to pay attention. Notice the steppingstones. Notice the moments. Notice the things around me – what I had on my shelves and tables. What mattered.

Noticing is the first stage of creating those practices I need. But noticing is only the beginning. I have to be intentional as I move into the naming of those practices, taking them from my unconscious to conscious awareness.

Noticing is urgent but can't be rushed. Noticing requires my full presence. I notice the morning light as it brushes each heart in the stained-glass window that hangs outside our bedroom. The butterfly garden below that colorful glass spells abundance as seeds planted before the first frost emerge now as green shoots. I no longer remember what I planted where, so each delicate seedling is a surprise, a delight. In anticipation of monarchs and sulphurs, I have intermingled cornflowers and zinnias and milkweed with the dandelions already growing there. My eyes linger on the four hearts in the well-worn wedding window from my sister: the red heart lights up first, then gold, then yellow, and finally purple. The glass knows the ritual; each sunny day is the same.

Noticing takes time and demands showing up with my whole Self. Fortunately slow mornings are one of the great privileges of this time in my life. Not since the years before I started kindergarten have I had the luxury of moving leisurely as I start the day. Pace is a requisite to presence. And presence is essential to this journey. First I have to show up.

Naming is Power

My Five-Year-Old Self cowered at a reprimand from my father while riding my tricycle on a humid South Carolina morning alongside my neighbor Irwin, both of us in shorts with no shirt. Daddy named with loud certainty that girls' bodies were different from boys. I was not clear about the how, but I understood that I should be ashamed.

Naming carried a lot of weight for me. I learned early in life that naming is power. I grew up with Someone Else doing the naming for me, giving up not only my power, but confining my vision, restricting my possibility, shrinking my world.

Most of my life I wanted to be a boy. Well, not really most of my life. But I certainly wanted that from age 5 until about age 20 – and maybe even into my 30's... I not only wanted to be a boy; I yearned to be the son my father wanted. Awakening now to the promise of life at 75, to a freedom I have never known, I know what my Younger Self really wanted was to be seen. I wanted a voice. I wanted equal opportunities and rights, and I saw boys as having those privileges.

The power of Naming electrified my Thirty-Year-Old Self as the Women's Movement affected my life. I developed a strong sense of urgency to name before Someone Else did it for me, so sometimes I named too quickly, limiting my own possibilities, getting stuck in a box of my own making.

As I grasped the power of words, I became mired in my own anger and sense of overwhelm as I named as lies much of what I had accepted as truth. I had grown up in the segregated world of Charleston in the 1950's, with white and colored waiting rooms, white and colored water fountains, white and colored schools. My culture lifted up the naming of separate but equal as justification for racist structures. Now I found myself trapped in the muck of noticing that adults I trusted – parents and teachers and Girl Scout leaders and Sunday School mentors -- had lied to me.

Words mattered, and unlearning required reclaiming the power of Naming. That necessitated more noticing as I lived into the awareness that the lies were the only cultural paradigms those adults knew. And I shifted my anger and stuckness to renaming my work as moving beyond the cultural paradigms that I inherited and had been taught.

Nothing Left to Lose

Anger and resistance continue to be important teachers as I connect soul and role as Elder, and I am surprised that this work requires letting go. I know something about the cycles of separation and attachment, of the paradox of letting go and holding on, that mark the seasons of human life. But this feels like a different kind of letting go, of giving up the idea that resistance is negative, e.g., re-seeing the act of resisting arrest as a nonviolent way of claiming power; re-seeing the hierarchy's imposition of naming as my own opportunity for claiming authority by re-naming. I feel like I need more than courage to fully grasp that Elder means living into the realization that I have nothing left to lose. I lean into the words of singer Janis Joplin and writer Kris Kristofferson.

Freedom's just another word for nothin' left to lose
Nothin' ain't worth nothin'
But it's free

I remember encircling myself with the words of Reinhold Niebuhr in my late teens:

Grant me the serenity to accept the things I cannot change,
the courage to change the things I can
and the wisdom to know the difference.

Niebuhr's concept of serenity allowed me to stand in my culture's insistence on the status quo as I struggled to find ways of living with what I knew was wrong or at least debatable. But I needed several more decades of exposure to the Civil Rights Movement and the Women's Movement to embrace the words of Angela Davis:

I am no longer accepting the things
I cannot change.
I am changing the things I cannot accept.

My learning and unlearning continue. In the past decade, Supreme Court Justice Ruth Bader Ginsburg has been one of my sheroes, a vital role model and Elder in my life. Her reminder to fight for the things I care about, but to do it in a way that will lead others to join me, deepens my ability to hold paradox. My anger evolves into energy and passion.

Intermezzo

After Reading Alice Walker's
There is a Flower at the End of My Nose
Smelling Me

My work is connecting:

Being the bridge, being the thread,

Being the rope from the back door;

    Wanting to help a wanderer lost in a blizzard,

    A wonderer lost in thought,

        Find the way home.

Here the teacher, here the student,

Here the flower, here the seed.

    Sometimes moving, sometimes still.

    Sometimes alone, sometimes surrounded,

        Always interconnected.

The mockingbird sings the Beauty

He loves, the gardenia fills

The Air with her Beauty.

    I let the Beauty I love

    Be what I do,

        Reciprocating in my human way.

--Sally Z. Hare

Notes to Me

I felt the warm sun of Bali as I tried to listen respectfully despite my overwhelming jetlag; the warmth only increased my desire to curl up in a ball and sleep. My extreme tiredness after a 23-hour flight enhanced my sense of having been transported into a fantasy world, a kaleidoscope of foreign sounds and colors.

Surya, our guide and host for this two-week tumble into the healing arts through the lens of Balinese culture, insisted the market be our first stop as we left the airport. I attempted to be responsive or at least polite as the heaviness of my eyelids threatened to shut down my brain. The unidentifiable smells and clatters and tones created havoc with my efforts to separate reality from a sense of the mystical.

As I followed Surya's directions to shop for a sarong to wear to temple to show respect, I was invited into conversation by the shopkeeper. The petite woman with few teeth and graying hair and caramel-colored smooth skin put me at ease as she showed me how to wrap the cotton batik material. Her English was better than my Balinese, but that wasn't saying much as we both struggled to communicate. I admired the colors and designs in her fabrics, and then expressed my admiration for her children and their seeming comfort with strangers.

In fact, I was awed by the ease of the little ones at our feet as they slipped seamlessly from one language to another, chattering softly and translating for the adults. My arrogant American tourist perspective considered this culture as third world, and I, with a doctorate in early childhood, thought of myself as a bit of an expert in child development. Yet these Balinese youngsters defied my stereotypes.

"We see our children with soft eyes," the Balinese Elder explained to me. "Babies are holy. They have just come from God. We never leave a baby alone to cry. We never strike a baby. We don't let a baby touch the ground for her first year of life: ground dirty, baby holy. On child's first birthday, the whole community comes out to welcome her as her feet touch the ground for first time."

My foggy brain tried to make sense of it. No physical punishment. Comfort and attention to distress. That made sense... But soft eyes...

I asked again: "Please help me understand soft eyes."

The woman smiled knowingly, betel-nut-stained teeth evident. "It's like when you're in love. It's not that you don't see the sharp edges and flaws of the person you're in love with, but your eyes are coated with love that blurs those edges. Like Vaseline on your camera. Everything looks softer."

Mystery: My Story

The memory floods me as I write now about connecting soul and role as Elder, as I grasp that my life is not my story. My story is the way I create meaning.

My culture has always valued story; we treat **his** story – history – as gospel, as the **True** or Real story.   The Women's Movement has shifted that paradigm for some of us, as we have claimed **her** story – herstory – and have begun to tell new stories, more inclusive ones. I smile as I think if his story is history and her story is herstory, then my story is mystery. And I know that soft eyes are necessary, not only for Others but for my Self as I construct meaning.

Steppingstone to Portal

My Sankofa guide accompanied me as I looked back and   remembered my love of learning, my love of teaching. The first in my family to go to college, I was well aware of my family's skepticism of the necessity for this venture for a female, but there was no question in **my** mind. That early steppingstone of kindergarten was the portal to finding my passion for teaching and learning, to uncovering that birthright gift.

My Five-Year-Old Self didn't wait to grow up: I created a school in our living room for my sisters and neighborhood children. I intuitively knew the interconnectedness of play and learning. Much later I learned that educator Maria Montessori had named play as the child's work. Early childhood educator Erika Christakis called play the "defining feature" of all mammalian development, denoting that its "signature" was apparent in the bodies and lives of children who experience it:

(Children's) life expectancies are longer and their social-emotional capabilities are more robust when they have a chance to learn through play and deep relationships, and when their developing brains are given the chance to grow in a nurturing, language-rich, and relatively unhurried environment.

-- Christakis in a 2019 interview with Edutopia, the online presence of the George Lucas Foundation

Looking back, I recognized that my young students were important teachers for me. In my college classes, I embraced the ideas of Friedrich Froebel and his vision of what he named the kindergarten; literally a garden for children, a place in which they can flower into the blossoms they came to be. I understood play to be equally important in the lives of adults – and often a portal to spiritual unfolding and wholeness. Whether working with four-year-olds or graduate students, I understood my role as teacher meant noticing the seeds of True Self in my students. My job was to mirror those seeds and encourage the students to name their gifts, while I nurtured each seed with everything within my power to offer the best chance for blooming.

Public education too often did not support and respect me as a teacher – nor was there much acknowledgement or support for the necessity for creativity and lifetime learning. I wanted to change that, not only for myself – but for the children in the system. I recognized, early in my career, my role in changing a very entrenched structure; my young Teacher Self decided the best way to change the system was to transform teacher education. Graduate school was never a goal but a portal to changing the things I did not accept.

The gift of meeting Parker J. Palmer in the early 1990's was another steppingstone-to-portal as Parker's clarity about living undivided and his invitation to pilot the work of The Courage to Teach affirmed my path. My brain sizzled with excitement as my heart resonated with Parker's knowing that we teach who we are.

Returning to early memories, I see now that I learn by teaching. For me, *teacherlearner* is one word; I can't separate them. Now I want to create fruitful ground and the chance to blossom for my Self and others in the ElderGarten. And I want to change the system that doesn't recognize our need for Elders and that denigrates and demeans the journey.

The Beauty I Love

Rumi has long instructed me to let the beauty I love be what I do. Only now, as the first flower of the season smiles down at me from just above my head, do I understand the beauty I love as a practice that deepens my resilience to continue on this journey.

I gently pull the branch down to cutting level. Pink doesn't do it justice. Maybe one of those lipstick names: Creamy Rose or Simply Salacious Cherry or Deep Velvet Crimson or Glowing Sunrise.

This now-six-foot bush barely reached my knees on that desolate December day I brought it home after leaving the courthouse. My divorce was final. Six years and two months from marriage ceremony to divorce decree. My Twenty-Something Self, already in a dark hole in the holiday season, wanted some kind of ritual, a ceremony to mark the end of what I thought would be happily-ever-after.

I didn't regret the marriage. Or the divorce. I felt some fear and apprehension about how I would cope financially, realizing I probably would need to sell the house. In many ways my marriage was an education in men (or at least one member of the species) after growing up in a family of girls. I was grateful for the glimpses into male vulnerability and the ways in which, like females, males are deformed by cultural expectations. The one that surprised me the most was the retardation of emotional intelligence, warped by a culture that preached men could only show anger, never fear or grief.

My marriage also freed me from many cultural expectations, not the least of which were the roles of wife and husband. Growing up in the 1950's and 60's, I saw on television and in my textbooks the stereotyped wife who cleaned the kitchen in high heels and a frilly apron --- and paradoxically, I heard the voices of Betty Friedan and Gloria Steinem and Dorothy Pitman Hughes and Shirley Chisolm encouraging me to think outside of those patriarchal boxes.

Encouraged by our young marriage to feel safe in trying on new ways of being, I know now that the culture didn't offer my young husband the same support. Our families couldn't offer what they didn't have. Looking back, I recognize the sense that we could be more together than we were separately had been eroded by everyday exposure to a world that sent us both into scarcity, into fear of losing our Selves.

I went to the courthouse alone on that dreary December day. There was no reason for anyone else to be there for this uncontested ending. It took all of five minutes for the judge to declare the divorce final – and for me to affirm that there was no property settlement or anything else to be decided by the court. We each came to the marriage with very little, agreeing to split equally anything we had acquired. That included the house and everything in it; I was grateful that he didn't want the dog.

In some ways the divorce was a relief, so wanting a ritual, a sense of closure, was unexpected. My car seemed to go to the nearest nursery of its own accord; I had never been there before. I walked around, drawn to the camellias with petals of sunset. I bought a small camellia bush that had two rose-like blooms and several buds.

When nothing else flowers in the winter, the camellia stands out in Southern gardens. When that camellia blooms from her now-towering height, she affirms the choices that young woman made almost fifty years ago. She reminds me of my resilience and ability to keep the house, not to mention my life. She reminds me that it takes a really good husband to be better than none. Her months of winter flowers reflect my own resilience.

Intermezzo

Stepping Stones

"I have always thought of poems as stepping stones in one's own sense of oneself."

--Seamus Heaney

I like that notion
Of poems
As stepping stones,

As first ways
Of hearing
My Self, my own inner voice.

London Bridge
Is falling down,
Falling down.

Mary's lamb,
It was against
The rule.

Jack Horner's plum:
Oh what a good boy
Am I.

I'm nobody,
Who are you?
Are you nobody too?

There there's a pair of us.
Jack and Jill
Falling, falling

In Flanders Field
The poppies grow
And the daffodils at Ashley Hall

And the azaleas
Ablaze in Hampton Park
While phlox grow wild on Sullivans Island.

This year is yours;
It has not long to stay
So make the most

Of each important
Day moment breath
Memory

Horse-drawn cortege
Little John-John
Standing at attention

So much to come:
Stepping stones
For life.

--Sally Z. Hare

Notes to Me

We come into the world as whole human beings. All the seeds of True Self are present in the infant. As children and young adults, we deny our gifts, feeling they are not valuable because they are ours. Religion and education are powerful institutions in shaping the young person's sense of feeling divided, creating the need to wear masks; to put on, in the words of May Sarton, other people's faces.

> *Now I become myself. It's taken*
> *Time, many years and places;*
> *I have been dissolved and shaken,*
> *Worn other people's faces...*

Now I Become Myself, from *Collected Poems, 1930-1993*

As we move towards becoming an Elder, we seek the safe spaces where we may safely remove the masks and claim our true faces. Many of the steppingstones along the way are those people and places that offer insight to our authentic Selves, glimpses of the wholeness that is our birthright.

Beauty as a Steppingstone

I lift up the tiny silver turtle to dust the dresser --- and get stopped by a memory so strong I catch my breath. The turquoise stone in its head draws me every bit as much as it did the first day I saw it in a Charleston antique store with my mother and grandmother when I was five or six.

My grandmother Ida loved antique shopping, especially for mismatched sterling spoons for her silver collection. She never required things to match – whether on the table or on her person. The palette of furniture and pillows and art in her living room and parlor were a colorful garden. Why would you plant only red tulips or yellow daffodils when you could delight in the whole bouquet?

The small dark object in the case was just at my eye level. Barely three inches from nose to tail, the turtle stood out to me among the larger and heavier vases and pieces of jewelry. Ida politely asked Mr. Hildebrandt, standing in his leather apron behind the counter, to let us have a closer look.

In the palm of my hand, the turtle's shell delighted me with an even larger turquoise stone, surrounded by shiny green emeralds. His head wiggled as I touched him. Mr. Hildebrandt came from behind the counter to reveal a secret compartment with a tiny mirror and a perfectly-rounded velvety yellow powder puff.

"In the old days," the gentle store owner told me, "a lady might attend a ball at a very elegant place. She would carry this compact in her handbag; then she might open it in the ladies' room and discreetly powder her nose so it wouldn't shine."

I loved the way he talked to me like a grown-up, expecting that I would understand. The turtle was becoming more of a treasure each moment.

"How much?" my grandmother asked.

"$20."

Even before my mother objected, I knew that was expensive. "Mother, she doesn't need that."

"How can she grow up to love beautiful things if she doesn't have them?" asked Ida, as she pulled the bills from her purse. Mr. Hildebrandt carefully wrapped the little creature in tissue and put it in a small bag.

"I don't think it's sterling," my grandmother said to my mother as we walked the car. "But I hope it will be the first of many things to catch her attention simply because they are beautiful. I want her to understand that beauty needs no reason, no justification. I hope she will always open her hands and heart to welcome the beauty that she loves."

Seventy years later I lift the tiny turtle to dust the dresser. I open the bottom of its shell, transported to another place, another time. The mirror has some dark spots around its edges – and the puff has been lost in some unknown place. I feel the same joy, the same delight, the same awe – and I thank Ida for the gift of beauty as a steppingstone, a portal, into this journey of a lifetime.

The Seed Corn

In second grade

Miss Mason gave us

Each a Dixie cup,

Our names printed

In her flawless manuscript.

With the perfection and concern

Unique to seven-year-olds,

We poked in the bottom

Three pencilpoint holes before

Miss Mason poured sloooowly

The black storebought

Dirt for our counting-out-loud

One-two-three indentations

With our pinky fingers.

I remember the care

To this day,

The precision of

Those three holes.

Three corn kernels:

Bright yellow precious

Hard foreign coins of

Gold on our desktops,

One for each hole.

Miss Mason demonstrated

How to cover our seeds,

To carefully water

From a tiny pitcher,

To place just so

In the window's light.

What a sight those

Dixie cups lining the sill,

Twenty-seven little soldiers

In red-white-blue

Standing at attention

Waiting, waiting

For what seemed like forever

But was probably only three days

Until Harriett spotted a spike

Of green in her cup.

The first. Then they started: Marty's

And Suzanne's. Stanley's and Buddy's.

Even the slow readers and the ones

Bad at math had at least two

If not three green stems.

Mine took forever; it really did,

One of the last to poke

Through the dirt.

But half a century later

The memory still gleams.

And I am still

Planting seeds.

                    ---Sally Z. Hare

The Day the Rain Came

My hunger to learn to read was stronger than my painful shyness. Somehow I understood, even as a young child, that learning was social, that I needed a community to learn. That morning started in the usual way, with the pledge of allegiance. My first-grade teacher was a World War II veteran who honored the flag as an important member of our class. Attendance and lunch money collection were standard parts of the morning ritual before our reading groups could begin.

I was patient but anticipatory as Miss Mason called the Robins to the circle. That was the signal to leave our desks and join the teacher in the front of the classroom, taking our places on the sturdy short wooden chairs that formed a circle with Miss Mason's tall chair. A perfect triangle of light from the autumn sun marked the center as we sat in the Reading Circle, opening our books to the right page, getting ready to decode the letters, the sounds.

Whether Robins or Cardinals or Wrens, we all loved to move to the Reading Circle, to be with Miss Mason as we learned the vowels, long and short, and most of the consonants. Each day since the beginning of school, we had written another rule in our black composition books. The rules held magic, a promise of becoming a reader; my favorite was the one about when two vowels went walking, the first did the talking.

On this fall morning we practiced blending the sounds. I noticed Miss Mason's yellow dress, smiling to myself as I noted her looking more like a canary than a robin. I longed to please her, to make her smile; I wanted to **be** her. My stomach hurt with that tension every time The Robins were summoned to the front of the class.

"Sound out the letters. Remember the Rules. And when you think you know the Word, raise your hand – and I will let you whisper in my ear."

I tried SO hard. I knew the sounds of the consonants

r and *n*. I raised my hand, and the teacher beckoned me up to whisper. No, she shook her head – and I slid sadly into my seat. I tried again. And again. Each time Miss Mason sent me back to my small chair in the circle. By now, Stanley and Harriet and Hank were all standing with smug smiles of whispered Rightness.

Suddenly the letters seemed to slide together into the sun's triangle: *r-r-r-r*... Long *a*.. Oh, yes, the *i* was silent: when two vowels go walking, the first does the talking.

N...n...n... r-A-n, rain, I whispered.

Miss Mason smiled and nodded – and I joined the others, the sun-triangle touching the toe of my black patent Mary Janes. Nothing was the same after **rain** came. I was becoming a Reader with this steppingstone of decoding letters into sounds into words. (For years my ability to decode exceeded my ability to comprehend, but adults were still impressed!)

I had discovered the beauty I loved, the thread with which I would weave connectedness for everything I needed for this journey to becoming an Elder. Becoming a Reader was indeed my magical portal.

That portal unlocked my birthright gift for learning. I wanted to read everything. Reading became my preferred form of play: reading to my little sisters, reading to my dolls, and best of all, reading to my Self. I also wanted to share my newly-found passion by teaching others to read. Looking back, I can see the connectedness of my discovery of reading with my career choice and my preferred way of learning for a lifetime.

I am a reader: a reader who learns, a reader who writes, a reader who cooks, a reader who plays piano, a reader who gardens, a reader who teaches. Reading is my doorway to everything. So of course, I am distressed when the Sufi poet Rumi, already an important steppingstone, now cautions against reading:

> *Don't open the door to the study*
> *and begin reading.*
> *Take down a musical   instrument.*
> *Let the beauty we love be what we do.*
> *There are hundreds of ways to kneel*
> *and kiss the ground.*

Of course I will begin reading: that IS the beauty I love. I take longer to understand Rumi's wisdom that there are hundreds of ways to kneel and kiss the ground, that **my** Beauty may not be yours.

As I pay attention to the beauty I love and become more intentional about honoring that beauty in my life, I remember --- and discover --- and uncover --- my own birthright gifts. With Sankofa on my shoulder, I recognize that I have known of birthright gifts since early childhood from the fairy tales I inhaled.

I remember my favorite story of Sleeping Beauty –
and the important description of the fairies naming
her birthright gifts, from musical talent to a kind
disposition. My Sankofa companion now opens
my eyes to the portal from that steppingstone, the
knowing that environment plays an important role in
how genetic gifts get nurtured – or don't -- as another
fairy steps in to say the child will prick her finger and
die. As all the fairies in attendance gasp in despair, a
possibility opens when another fairy says she doesn't
have the power to change the course of events and stop
the fingerprick-- but she can turn the death sentence
into a long sleep.

Once again I recognize my love of reading as the
connection between these steppingstones in my life –
and I glimpse that beauty I love as the magic that allows
portals to emerge from many of those steppingstones.

Of Grief and Play and Creativity

When a hurricane took out a huge growth of trees in
our backyard, the depth of our grief surprised us. As
I spent time with the beauty of the remaining trunks, I
found myself envisioning a fairy garden in that space. I
planted flowers in the crevasses – and enjoyed making
houses and small creatures. Squirrels and birds helped
by planting seeds of their own, and friends and family
members brought gifts of fairies and gnomes.

A sense of play and creativity grew in that space

between the loss of our trees and our grief. The garden has continued to grow and change for the past several years, and this year some saplings are growing out of those fallen trunks. The fairy garden is evolving into a fairy forest – and I am regaining my relationship with the natural world in a way I haven't known since kindergarten.

It seems obvious as I write these words, but in recovering my love for all that lives in my yard, I find a sense of mutuality and reciprocity that is essential to uncovering my hidden wholeness. Of course, I love nature and the beauty of the plants and beach and birds and bugs, but I have been deformed by cultural paradigms into naming a dividedness between humans and things, whether grasses or dragonflies or peonies or the marsh.

There is no quick fix; I have much unlearning to do to reclaim my kinship with all of earth as I connect soul and role as Elder. I am grateful for the trees-turned-fairy-garden-turning trees-again that are my portal.

The steppingstone of the loss of the trees has opened into a portal. Reading what I am writing in this field guide gives me the awareness that steppingstones from my lifetime journey have the potential to become portals when I return to reflect on that experience in ways that allow me to make meaning and bring what has been unconscious into consciousness. When a portal opens, I have the opportunity to name the practices that will allow me to intentionally nurture what I am noticing.

As I travel back into the memories, I feel mired in the messiness of many threads in my lifetime and the struggle to hold onto those threads. I recall the words of poet William Stafford's *The Way It Is*:

There is a thread you follow.

And I hear in my head his stern warning:

Nothing you do can stop times unfolding.
But you don't ever let go of the thread.

An intense awareness hits me: I must do more than follow those threads and even more than never letting go of them. Weaving those threads is the essence of meaning-making.

The inner work of weaving allows the interconnectedness of so many of the steppingstones on my journey to become visible. That is when I turn to the practices that deepen my resilience for that work of finding my hidden wholeness, of becoming an Elder.

I am also seeing the interrelatedness of my practices. As I notice what I have named, I find myself weaving and interweaving those ways of being, revealing another practice I need now: moving beyond the cultural paradigms that no longer serve me.

Intermezzo

A Woman's Garden of Verse

the purple pansy face greets me

as I pick up the morning news,

its gentle sweetness an antidote

to the daily bomb scares and rapes.

i'm grateful for the soft smell

of pansies in the morning,

velvet optimism in the early light.

--Sally Z. Hare

Notes to Me

The last of life, for which the first was made. Those words from the poet Robert Browning entered my Teenage Self in my freshman English class; my almost-eighteen-year-old heart absorbed the words with a glimmer of another steppingstone on the journey to become an Elder.

The words stayed with me through the next decades as I lived into the meaning. Along the way I was also drawn by the words of   T. S. Eliot's *Four Quartets*, "We had the experience but missed the meaning." I puzzled for years before knowing that I didn't miss the meaning; I wasn't ready for the meaning. We can't see what we don't know.

Creating the Meaning

I remember pondering over Eliot's words about "the approach to the meaning restoring the experience in a different form." Now I know that my work has never been about restoring the meaning, but rather finding or discovering and finally creating the meaning. This amazing voyage towards connecting soul and role as an Elder, this work of being Human, is all about meaning.

And meaning is very personal, very intimate. Only I can make sense of my journey – and it's too hard to do alone. Humans are social creatures; we are hard-wired to connect. My life is entangled with everyone and everything around me. I need help to see it, to be it, to make sense of it. Of course, I need practices that enable me to stay the course as I construct the meaning of my life in ways that offer joy and contentment and challenge and clarity as I stand here at 75.

My husband Jim has been an important partner and role model and companion, affirming that creating meaning is both a privilege and a responsibility. Jim talks about "response-ability" as responding with ability as he, at age 88, does his work of reflecting and constructing meaning. He explains in "Letting Go" in his poetry book, *Looking Around:*

Dreams. I had a few.
Wanted to be a cowboy and ride horses
shoot guns, kill bad guys be
the hero of my life.
I had to let go of that.

Wanted to be the quarterback make
touchdowns win exciting games, get the girls,
get lifted up as a
champion all-star.
I had to let go of that.

Wanted to be a great lover, with long
conquest lists, play the field for all it was
worth before finding the most beautiful wife
to be mine forever.
I had to let go of that.

Wanted to be a Hollywood star, admired by
the world, with fan club magazine
covers, the most cheered acceptance
speech for Oscar.
I had to let go of that.

Wanted that perfect family, with that perfect
wife, perfect gender children, beautiful home
in the best neighborhood driving the most
expensive car on the block.
I had to let go of that.

Wanted a vacation home, on the lake in the
mountains with an inboard motor boat a dock
with water sports excellent restaurants near-
by and envious neighbors.
I had to let go of that.

Instead

*I got to be a respected accountant, an effective
 lineman, a shy woman-magnet, the president
of Kiwanis, owner of a mortgage free home in
the nice suburbs, a Subaru, after one divorce, a
perfect wife with intelligence and beauty, four
unequaled children, two of each, all college
graduates, and was voted volunteer of the year
when I was 70.*

I hold on tight to all that.

Seed to Seed

In my early childhood classrooms, I often planted seeds in Dixie cups with my children as I remembered my teacher's doing with me. I created multiple spaces for them to glimpse that seeds are the first stage of life, requiring darkness to be born – and light to grow. We celebrated as the final stage the plant's blooming. I thought the flower, the fruit, ended the cycle.

But I was wrong.

Now I know that returning to seed is the final stage. And my culture reviles the notion of going to seed. Our language that describes producing seed is often negative and disrespectful. As I return to seed, I not only want to embrace this stage of life – but I want to celebrate that knowing with others.

In the ElderGarten, we intentionally notice and name that our life cycle not only begins with the seeds of True Self, but also ends with seeds of True Self, legacy seeds. Nurturing the practice of seed to seed means developing the seeds that hold our birthright gifts and valuing and honoring those seeds that we spread and disburse and plant as our legacy.

I thought the role of Elder was the ending, just as I mistakenly thought the flower was the ending. Now I am coming to see that Elder may be the work before the Work of becoming an Ancestor. There is an important difference in those roles. I can commit to living into the role of Elder; whether or not I reach that place of Ancestor is in the hands, or perhaps the eyes and hearts, of those who follow me.

In addition I am learning that my legacy is my story, not only how I tell it but how I share it and place it with care in the hands and hearts of those who follow me. In one of my favorite movie scenes at the end of *Camelot*, King Arthur knights young Tom, after the boy insists that he knows all the wondrous tales of the King and his Round Table. Then Arthur sends the boy away from the battlefield, commanding him to return home and tell everyone those stories.

King Pellinor interrupts the king:
"Arthur, what are you doing?
You have a battle to fight!"

Arthur replies,
"I have won my battle, Pelli. What we did,
will be remembered."
Arthur turns to Tom: "Now run, Sir Tom, behind the lines."

As Tom runs towards home, King Pellinor asks,
"Arthur, who was that?"
King Arthur: "One of what we all are, Pelli.
Less than a drop in the great blue motion
of the sunlit sea.
But it seems that some of the drops sparkle, Pelli.
Some of them do
sparkle."
"Run, Boy! Run, boy! Run! Oh, run, my boy!"

Arthur's words to the disappearing lad are a steppingstone for me, elucidating my responsibility to share my story, to seed and water my legacy.

As I travel this path, I gain insight that my legacy is more than telling my story. It's more than sharing my story. It is also about creating a space for others to bring their stories into consciousness.

My wise friend Elaine Sullivan, licensed counselor and marriage and family therapist and co-founder of the Center for Renewal and Wholeness, is my greatest teacher in that. More than 50 years ago, Elaine encouraged her community college students, women in their 30's and 40's and 50's, to claim their voices by writing their stories. She is a pioneer in our understanding of the power of story:

> *Beneath the story we know consciously is another story that propels our lives. Making the unconscious part of our story more conscious is life work. In these written stories the evidence of that deep inner work is ever present, the work of listening to our own inner teacher, the work of recovering our True Self. Our stories are written in the biology of our bodies and give us clues to our personal conditioning in mind, body and spirit -- clues to who I am.*
>
> --Elaine Sullivan in "The Song in My Heart,"
> *The Story Mandala*

As I connect soul and role as Elder, I grasp the importance of consciously making memories. I realize that so many of my memories were created unconsciously with no intent that I would remember. My husband Jim R. Rogers, in his book *The Incredible Importance of Effective Parenting*, points to intentional memory-making as one of a parent's most important duties:

"What kind of memories are you creating?"

Money Consciousness

As this Reader writes, I am discovering threads in my story by reading my own words. Being intentional as I move from noticing to naming, moving from unconsciousness (or perhaps what Jung named as pre-consciousness) to consciousness, I awaken even more on this journey to connecting soul and role as Elder. I surprise my Self with the realization that I have been unconscious of money for much of life.

Going back again and again with my Sankofa guide, I uncovered many negative cultural messages about women and money from my youth and in the post-World War II world that championed capitalism and consumerism and material consumption. As I took out memories and examined them, I was continually startled by my unconsciousness about money and my lack of awareness that how I earned it and spent it was related to my values.

I turned to my friend and mentor Megan LeBoutillier's writing:

Much of what we tell ourselves about money is a lie, or a justification for wrongdoing. We give money more meaning than life, the natural world, and even ourselves. Many people will do almost anything to garner more money. We pollute for money. We kill for money, and we disregard our souls when it comes to money. We live in a culture that encourages us to do this. Unless we admit this and shift our consciousness regarding money, we will forever operate without conscious awareness. We need to become familiar with our values, our assumptions and our world views when it comes to financial matters.

- The Mobius Flow of Money

I name the practice of money consciousness as I move with intention from what Megan names as society's norm of silence and scarcity to one of confidence and sufficiency. Jacob Needleman's words resonate with my knowing that nurturing money consciousness is essential to uncovering my hidden wholeness:

Without consciousness of the part of ourselves that is involved with money, we run the risk of becoming moral or spiritual beings with only one half of our nature—and therefore not really moral or spiritual at all.

--Needleman, *Money and the Meaning of Life*

I am still in the process of unlearning, but I am clear

that money consciousness is vital as I consider legacy at this stage in becoming an Elder. I see again the entanglement of my practices as I once again pick up the beloved turtle compact. Now my Sankofa companion shows me that the steppingstone is not only about the beauty I love, but also a peek into money consciousness. Ida's gift to me that day holds a glimpse into money as integrity, of taking it into the outer world in a way that reflects my inner knowing. Money doesn't only buy things; it offers a way of bringing my Inner Self into the outer world in very material ways.

Money is entangled for me with another of the practices: hope. As I claim my voice to tell my story and construct the meaning of my life, I see that money has often represented hope for me – whether I was giving it or receiving it. Money has the capacity to create cracks where the Light gets in if, as Megan writes, money flows.

> **Everything has a crack in it.**
> **That's how the Light gets in.**
> --Leonard Cohen, *Anthem*

As I continue to embrace the journey towards wholeness, I am noticing more and more cracks where the Light gets in. I name those cracks as hope --- and I need practices to nurture that hope in a world where the cracks are seemingly harder to detect. I need the practice of hope to deepen my resilience, my energy, my sense of aliveness.

Hope is NOT an idealistic state of seeing the world through rose-colored lenses. Perhaps the best definition is Emily Dickinson's:

"Hope is the thing with feathers."

Mary Oliver tells us to "Keep some room in your heart for the unimaginable." My knowing now is that if I can keep that room in my heart as I notice the steppingstones, I create portals for moving from unimaginable to possible. My Mother used to tell me that some things have to be believed to be seen; that requires the practice of hope.

I accept the responsibility of nurturing hope as a vital part of my role as Elder. A few years ago, I decided to begin the New Year by posting something hopeful on Facebook. I never intended to make that a practice, but the act of noticing hope in order to post it daily on Facebook has increased my capacity for finding it. I have continued for more than four years – and others respond with gratitude and with their own signs of hope.

Nurturing this practice of hope has allowed my heart to break open into greater capacity for wholeness, for sustaining the journey to becoming an Elder. I am again aware of the entanglement of my practices, that they are not separate as I move from my Inner Self to my Outer World. When I practice hope, I recognize my being part of something larger.

No Ending in a Mobius Strip

I am still trying to find an ending, even as I know that there IS no ending. The journey is not linear; it is a seamless flow. There are no endings.

We come into the world knowing that what we need is here. We are born into community, interconnected to everything in the Universe. Quantum physics now confirms the undivided wholeness into which every child is born and affirms our innate sense that we **are** community.

During youth and childhood we too often lose sight of our connectedness; cultural paradigms and rigid perspectives get in the way, and we forget. Finding it again is the work of a lifetime. Finding it again is the work of becoming an Elder, of connecting soul and role.

Parker Palmer often uses the image of the Mobius strip, a continuous curve, to illustrate that continuous stream. His words come back to me now as I seek an image to represent this non-linear journey:

Whatever is inside of us continually flows outward, helping to form or deform the world — depending on what we send out. Whatever is outside us continually flows inward, helping to form or deform us — depending on how we take it in. Bit by bit, we and our world are endlessly re-made in this eternal inner-outer exchange.

You can easily create a Mobius strip by taking a paper strip and giving it a half-twist, and then joining the ends of the strip together to form a loop. Parker  writes in *A Hidden Wholeness* that *"we are constantly engaged in a seamless exchange between whatever is out there and whatever is in here, co-creating reality, for better or for worse."*

Habits of the Heart

The cultural messages that surround me make the journey to becoming an Elder more difficult. Once again I am affirmed in my strong knowing that I need practices to deepen my courage and strength to stay on this path, especially with the many voices around me that disparage and discount my commitment.

I have not let myself slip into the illusion that I could create these practices before living them, before noticing what is emerging. I intentionally have spent time – days, weeks, months, years – noticing and naming what gives me energy, what makes me feel alive, as well as what takes me to a place of feeling stuck or unable to move. I have tried on other people's practices – and practices from books and workshops and classes and wisdom traditions, giving myself permission to name what I was noticing – and then to change the name if it no longer fit.

I am noticing and want to name the paradox of practices:

they are personal. What I need may not be what you need. Effective practices are intimately individual; there is no one size fits all. Practices are also not etched in stone; they are not rigid and may change over time. What I need in my 20's may not be what I need in my 40's, in my 70's...

I name these practices with the intention of nurturing the kind of space, for my Self and for others, that is deliberately different from what we too often experience as normal. I am pointing the way to that field in which we have the best chance to live an undivided life, a life of wholeness, a life of integrity; Rumi's field that is beyond wrongdoing and rightdoing.

My emergent practices have shown up throughout this field guide, and you are welcome to take those that speak to you, even as you begin to name your own. I am very aware that these intentional ways of being in the world are dynamic and energetic and may change over time. Some may leave... Or others may join them. On some days one practice may be more important than another. In the first pages, I shared with you my knowing that the practices are not linear, so rather than making a list, I have offered them through my stories and asked you to read in circles. I have also gathered the practices at the close of the field guide, so you could find them in one place for reference as you begin to name your own practices.

As I nurture these ways of being, I realize they are

becoming habits of the heart. I again turn to the wisdom of my friend Parker J. Palmer in *Healing the Heart of Democracy:*

"Habits of the heart"
(a phrase coined by Alexis de Tocqueville)
are deeply ingrained ways of seeing, being,
and responding to life that involve our minds,
our emotions, our self-images, our concepts of
meaning and purpose.

Naming these practices has been my work before the Work; now nurturing these evolving habits of the heart becomes essential as I coddiwomple toward wholeness, moving forward, looking backward, nurturing my seed of True Self.

Journey of a Lifetime

I always enjoyed watering Aunt Gussie's flowers in her sunroom – and Ida's succulents on the porch above the hardware store. Sometimes I'd pop off a thick leaf of the hens-and-chickens and pretend to paint the banisters.

Picking Aunt Bertie's pansies was another favorite pastime. "Take all you want," she'd say, showing us how to snap the stem. "The more you pick, the more they grow."

Now I have my own cutting garden. After forty-nine years of tending and planting in the same spot, the flowers bloom in all seasons. Arranging fresh bouquets for the bedroom brings such joy as I let the beauty I love be what I do.

"Friends don't let friends buy annuals," says the T-shirt my friend Sandie gave me. Yet even some annuals are returning for another season in this climate-changed environment. Sweet William and begonias have come back this year, after spending the winter underground. I let go of old patterns and delight in planting seeds before the first frost, after the last frost, and every month between. The fairy and butterfly gardens show pinks and purples as delicate blossoms appear.

Annuals, perennials; roots, shoots; weeds, wildflowers; steppingstones, portals; lies, cultural paradigms; learning, unlearning: words matter, but naming is an infinite art. The beauty I love points the way to the ElderGarten. I live into the words of Jon Kabat -Zinn:

To drop into being means to recognize your interconnectedness with all life, and with being itself. Your very nature is being part of larger and larger spheres of wholeness.

I arrive now in the field beyond wrongdoing and rightdoing, content to drop into being as the meaning of my life whispers in the wind. In this field, I know my connectedness to all.

My life is not my story. My life is more than facts, more than steppingstones, more than memories. Sankofa is more than a metaphor; it is a responsibility. I will use my power to return:

San – to return

Ko – to go

Fa – to fetch, to seek and take.

I claim my authority to uncover my hidden wholeness as I connect soul and role as Elder.

This being human is the beginning and the end as we move from seed to seed in an infinitely delicious never-ending story. There is no happily ever-after. There is only this: embodying the beauty, embracing the absurdity of time, knowing the place as home. Mary Oliver's instructions for living come to mind:

Pay attention. Be astonished. Tell about it.

I let go of finding an ending as I enter the field of the ElderGarten. My work now is dispersing my seeds and weaving the threads. Creating my meaning. Offering the field guide. Living with integrity. Dancing with paradox. Sowing and sewing. Seeds and threads for the journey of a lifetime.

The Practices of The ElderGarten

Resilience grows out of practices that allow us to jump back
into our lives, our memories, our experiences, in order to
live into the role of Elder and discern the meaning of life.
I have shared those practices throughout this field guide
as they have emerged in my stories and memories. Now
I offer them here, acknowledging that they are not linear:
on any given day, one may be much more important than
another. I also realize that practices are very personal; there
is no one-size-fits-all. My hope is that you will take what
is useful and begin to notice that your own practices are
emerging.

• The Practice of Being Present

The practice of being present invites me into showing
up with my full Self. The practice of being present
requires breathing, which we sometimes forget to
do. The Latin word for breath is *spir*, allowing us to
glimpse the connectedness between breathing (outer
work) and spirit (inner work). Time does not exclude
past or future as we practice being present. Ram Dass
explains in *Be Here Now*: *"All the past and future —*
everything you always were is in this moment. All of your
commitments for the future are in this moment. The fullness

of this moment includes everything; it doesn't exclude. It doesn't exclude past and future. All we're dealing with is the problem that the human mind clings. The clinging of the human mind takes it into time and into space, and it takes it away from the fullness of the moment.... The reason the breath is so good to work with is it's always around, it's right there, and it's easy."

Being present is the work-before-the-Work of Presence. Elders exhibit Presence: a state of being that has the potential for intimacy and vulnerability, for inviting the Soul to show up fully in this transitory life. Presence is not a goal to be achieved, but rather, a way of living that comes from integrity, from undividedness between inner and outer. This kind of Presence is a paradox: it demands our attention and intention AND requires practice to let go of distractions. Multi-tasking and intrusions are intentionally set aside in the practice of being present.

• The Practice of Noticing, Naming, and Nurturing

Noticing requires being awake. Noticing takes time; it is too urgent to be rushed. It's about attention and intention and is interconnected with the practice of being present. Noticing is essential to the possibility of seeing our hidden wholeness: to arriving in the field in which, in Rumi's words, ideas, language, even the phrase *each other* doesn't make any sense.

Noticing is fundamental to naming. Deep listening and open, honest questions are essential elements of the work-before-the-Work in moving from noticing to naming. Names may change on this continual journey toward wholeness as labels or identifiers that worked earlier in the journey now no longer fit.

The attention and intention required for noticing become even more essential as we move from naming to nurturing. Nurturing entails consciously embodying what I have noticed and named as I move from my inner work into my outer world.

- **The Practice of Lifetime Learning and Unlearning: Moving Beyond Our Cultural Paradigms and Scarcity Mindset**

We are told we are human beings, not human doings; perhaps we are really human learnings. Research shows that humans begin learning in the womb and have the capacity to learn until the moment of death, and perhaps beyond.

Often our culture implies that learning is what happens in school – and life begins after graduation. The journey to becoming an Elder requires that we develop not only the practices of learning for a lifetime, but also the value for lifelong learning. Unlearning is often an important aspect of those practices. Moving beyond the cultural paradigms of our youth and childhood frequently requires unlearning in order to open our minds to new ways of seeing, of being.

> *"It is what we know already that often prevents us from learning."*
>
> –Claude Bernard, French physiologist

A critical aspect of this practice is living from a place of abundance rather than scarcity; then moving beyond that paradox to the place of enoughness, of knowing that what we need is here.

> *what we need is here.*
> *And we pray, not for new earth or heaven,*
> *but to be quiet in heart, and in eye, clear.*
> *What we need is here.*
>
> ----Wendell Berry, Wild Geese
> from *Selected Poems of Wendell Berry*

• The Practice of Embracing Paradox

> *The opposite of a correct statement is a false statement.*
> *But the opposite of a profound truth*
> *may well be another profound truth.*
>
> - Niels Bohr, Danish physicist

A common cultural paradigm for many of us is to see things as contradictions, as either/or. When we embrace paradox, we deepen our understanding of what appear to be opposite poles, increasing our capacity to hold them as both/and.

...through all our lives we are faced with the task of reconciling opposites which, in logical thought, cannot be reconciled... How can one reconcile the demands of freedom and discipline in education? Countless mothers and teachers, in fact, do it, but no one can write down a solution. They do it by bringing into the situation a force that belongs to a higher level where opposites are transcended – the power of love... Divergent problems, as it were, force us to strain ourselves to a level above ourselves; they demand, and thus provoke, the supply of forces from a higher level, thus bringing love, beauty, goodness and truth into our lives.

---E. F. Schumacher, *Small is Beautiful*

• The Practice of Sankofa

The Sankofa bird is the symbol of the African proverb: **It is not taboo to go back and fetch that which you have forgotten**. As my metaphor and guide, this mythical bird holds a sacred seed in her beak, guarding and stewarding it with her life as she moves forward but looks backward.

That seed is the seed of True Self – and we can't know where we're going unless we know who we are and where we came from. This practice invites our moving fully into the work of remembering, slowing our pace to be able to travel ahead while looking behind – and inviting our knowing that we have choices in what we bring forward.

Allow your Self the privilege of remembering – and offer the gift of listening Self and others into memories. Respect (*re – spect*, from the Latin, to see again) the things (the photos, the knickknacks, the smells, the clothing, the songs, the "stuff" that hold memories) as well as the beliefs and hopes, the people and places, the dreams and realities, you have collected along the way. This practice allows us to make meaning of our story; to tell that story in my/y**our** voice.

*Those who do not have power over the story
that dominates their lives, the power to retell it, rethink
it, deconstruct it, joke about it, and change it as times
change, truly are powerless, because they cannot think new
thoughts.*

—Salman Rushdie

- ## The Practice of Letting the Beauty I Love Be What I Do

Today, like every other day, we wake up empty
and frightened. Don't open the door to the study
and begin reading. Take down a musical instrument.

Let the beauty we love be what we do. There are
hundreds of ways to kneel and kiss the ground.

---Rumi

The Beauty I love is a direct portal to remembering my birthright gifts and finding ways to take those gifts into the outer world. Yet sometimes I don't recognize or remember the Beauty I love. Letting the Beauty that I love be what I do makes me feel alive. The ability to see that Beauty is intricately entangled with some of the other practices, requiring noticing and naming and nurturing as well as dancing with the paradox of abundance and scarcity.

- ## The Practice of Living into the Thin Place between Loss and Grief

Loss is an existential element in human existence, even as our culture resists loss and its necessary partner, grief. Our first loss, whether it is a beloved blanket or a grandmother or a dog or the house we have always known or our parents' marriage, offers an important steppingstone on the journey towards wholeness. Yet our cultural paradigms around grief too often deny us entry into the thin place between grief and loss, that place where we are able to live into the paradox of love and loss and learn to hold both. That kind of heartbreak-into-healing is the gift to be received in that thin place between loss and grief.

• The Practice of Play

Play is the voice of the Inner Teacher who consistently and persistently invites us to be who we are, to be our authentic Selves. Play is a spiritual practice, even as it may also be physical and intellectual and emotional.

Play is the portal into creativity, allowing us to construct and deconstruct our world, empowering us to create our own meaning.

> *Play. Invent the World.*
> ---Salman Rushdie, *The Location of Brazil*

Albert Einstein calls play the highest form of research. After a career of studying play, Stuart Brown, M.D., founder of the National Institute for Play, writes in *Play: How It Shapes the Brain, Opens the Imagination, and Invigorates the Soul:*

(Play is) a force that has been built into us through millions of years of evolution, a force that allows us to both discover our essential selves and enlarge our world. We are designed to find fulfillment and creative growth through play.

76

- **The Practice of Money Consciousness**

Becoming conscious about money – and recognizing that how we use it in the outer world reflects our inner values -- is an essential part of connecting soul and role as an Elder. The practice of money consciousness enables me to move toward wholeness, away from what Megan LeBoutillier names as society's norm of silence and scarcity to a new paradigm of confidence and sufficiency. The practice is entangled with many of the other practices, from moving beyond cultural paradigms of what matters and of how I define legacy to hope as I recognize and enable the flow of money.

- **The Practice of Mutuality and Reciprocity in Our Relationship with the Natural World**

Until we reconcile our disconnectedness from our rightful place in Nature, we cannot live into wholeness. We must drop into being and reclaim interbeing, a term coined by the Buddhist monk Thich Nhat Hanh as a word to describe embracing our interdependence with everything. Connecting soul and role as Elder requires co-existing respectfully with all living things, being in right relationship with the living world around us.

Our sense of community and compassionate intelligence must be extended to all life forms, plants, animals, rocks, rivers, and human beings. This is the story of our past and it will be the story of our future.

- Terry Tempest Williams

Very much entangled with the practice of lifetime learning and moving beyond our cultural paradigms and scarcity mindset, this practice requires us to create a new story. Thomas Berry stresses the importance of that:

> *It's all a question of story. We are in trouble just now because we do not have a good story. We are in between stories. The Old Story — the account of how the world came to be and how we fit into it — is not functioning properly, and we have not learned the New Story.*

> *--Creative Energy: Bearing Witness for the Earth*

Shortly before he died, Berry was asked what advice he had for the next generations:

> *Tell them something new is happening,*
> *a new vision, a new energy, a new sacred story*
> *is coming into being in the transition from one era to another.*

- ## The Practice of Living Life from Seed to Seed

We often teach young children that the seed is the beginning of life. Rarely in our culture, do we acknowledge that the seed is also the last stage of life; that after the blossom and/or the fruit comes the seed.

Our cultural language about going to seed is often negative and disrespectful.

In the ElderGarten, we intentionally create the space to notice and name that our life cycle not only begins with the seeds of True Self, but also ends with seeds of True Self, legacy seeds – and that cycle repeats many times in a lifetime. An important part of this practice is nurturing the seeds that hold our birthright gifts – and valuing and honoring those seeds that we spread and disburse and plant after the blooming of our lifetime.

• The Practice of Hope

Hope is seeing the cracks in Leonard Cohen's *Anthem*: the cracks where the Light gets in. This practice invites us to believe that it's possible to emerge from this journey with our hidden wholeness becoming visible. The practice of hope allows our hearts to break open into greater capacity for healing and wholeness, for sustaining the journey to becoming an Elder.

As I end this section on the practices, I am again aware of the entanglement of these ways of being in the world. The practice of hope is entangled with the practice of noticing and naming and nurturing: the more I notice the cracks, the more Light I am able to name and nurture. The practice of hope invites us to see The Possible: some things have to be believed to be seen. Like the practice of being present, this practice is connected to the breath The Latin word for breath is *spir*, allowing us to glimpse the connectedness between breathing (outer work) and spirit (inner work).

Dum spiro spero.
While I breathe, I hope.

-Seal of the State of South Carolina

Words Matter:
The ElderGarten Glossary

glos·sa·ry: a collection of textual **gloss**es or of specialized terms with their meanings. The root word of glossary is **gloss,** a surface luster or brightness; shine.   **Merriam-Webster Dictionary, 2014**

Naming things is a political act, an act of power. So I am naming the things that are important in The ElderGarten – and sharing with you, the Reader, what I mean with the words I use. Words matter, and I want to be clear in my language.

I am refusing to give up words that are important to me because Others demean them or misuse them or label them as jargon. Instead I am claiming them here. As you read this Field Guide, my hope is that you will visit this glossary again and again; bathe in these names for things, delighting in knowing the meaning in **this** *context. I invite you to see the gloss of the words, the shine, the luster.*

birthright gifts: We come into this world as unique individuals, each with our own **birthright gifts**. They are hard for us to see, because they have always been there. Often if something comes easily for us, such as the gift to see with an artist's eye or the gift to remember poetry or the gift to see how to arrange a room with beauty, we devalue it. **Birthright gifts** are evident from the moment of birth; we only have to pay attention to an infant to understand that. Babies do not show up as raw material to be shaped by their environment and culture; they come fully formed, with the seed of true self. Yes, we are born with identity and integrity, and even as young children, we know what we like and dislike, what we are drawn towards and what we feel resistance to, what makes us feel alive and what drains our energy. But over the next decade or two, as we move through adolescence and schooling, we too often become **deformed**. We spend the first half of our lives abandoning our **birthright gifts**, Parker Palmer writes in *Let Your Life Speak*, or letting others disabuse us of them. The purpose of education, at its best, is to create the space for each of us to recognize and deepen our unique **birthright gifts**, to honor them and learn to use them in fulfilling our life's purpose.

Circle of Renewal and Wholeness®: The **Circle of Renewal and Wholeness®** is a registered trademark of the Center for Renewal and Wholeness, and the programs, grounded in the writing of Parker j. Palmer and decades of the storywork of Elaine Sullivan, can only be offered by facilitators prepared by the Center. Please see **Circle of Trust** (below) for a bit more.

Circle of Trust®, circle of trust: The **Circle of Trust®** is a registered trademark of the Center for Courage & Renewal, and the programs, grounded in the writing of Parker J. Palmer, can only be offered by facilitators prepared by the Center. I love that Parker also explains in *A Hidden Wholeness* that a **circle of trust** (spelled with lower case letters) could be two people or ten or twenty, who create a safe space for the soul to show up.

Coddiwomple: to travel forward in a purposeful manner towards an uncertain or unnamed destination.

Connecting Soul and Role; see Soul

Courage: From the Latin, *cor,* heart. Courage does not mean that we have no fear, but that we don't act out of that fear. See **heart**.

Courage Work: An affectionate way of talking about the various forms of Circles of Trust and Circles of Renewal and Wholeness (see above).

Elder: Elder is the time of Life when meaning blooms from a lifetime of seeds. An Elder lives with authenticity, with integrity. Elder is NOT synonymous with old person, though becoming an Elder is certainly the journey of a lifetime.

ElderGarten®: the field to grow into becoming an Elder. A space of play and joy; space for learning and opportunities for continued growth that is inner and outer; a space to notice and name and nurture the practices needed for resilience on the journey toward wholeness. Also a registered trademark of still learning, inc.

Hearing into speech: This wonderful way to describe a sacred deep listening that honors silence is credited to theologian Nelle Morton from her experiences in the early 1970's. She writes in *The Journey Is Home*, "If one can be heard to one's own speech, then the speech would be a new speech and the new speech would be a new experience in the life of the speaker – that is, the one heard to speech." She describes this kind of deep listening as "a depth hearing that takes place before speaking – a hearing that is more than acute listening. A hearing that is a direct transitive verb that evokes speech – new speech that has never been spoken before."

Heart: The heart is important in our journey to becoming an Elder, as it is literally where courage begins. The word courage comes from the Latin word for heart, **cor**. So we are reclaiming the word **heart** from its too-often sentimental use in our culture, to "the core of the self," as Parker writes in *Healing the Heart of Democracy*, "that center place where all ways of knowing converge – intellectual, emotional, sensory, intuitive, imaginative, experiential, relational, and bodily, among others. The heart is where we integrate what we know in our minds with what we know in our bones, the place where our knowledge can become more fully human."

Hidden wholeness: "There is in all things an invisible fecundity, a dimmed light, a meek namelessness, a hidden wholeness. This mysterious Unity, and Integrity, is Wisdom, the Mother of all, Natura naturans," writes Thomas Merton in *Hagia Sophia*. The journey to becoming an Elder, to connecting soul and role as Elder, allows that hidden wholeness to become visible.

Inner Teacher: The voice of the authentic Self in each of us; the voice that speaks of our Seeds of True Self, our birthright gifts. Thomas Merton calls it Wisdom (see Hidden Wholeness above).

Integrity: *Integrity*, from the Latin *integer* meaning whole or complete. In the context of becoming an Elder, integrity means connecting my Inner Self, my soul, with how I show up in my outer world, my role. Parker defines integrity in *The Courage to Teach*: "By **integrity** I mean whatever wholeness I am able to find within that nexus as its vectors form and re-form the pattern of my life. **Integrity** requires that I discern what is integral to my selfhood, what fits and what does not—and that I choose life-giving ways of relating to the forces that converge within me: do I welcome them or fear them, embrace them or reject them, move with them or against them? By choosing **integrity**, I become more whole, but wholeness does not mean perfection. It means becoming more real by acknowledging the whole of who I am."

Intermezzo: from the Italian, *mezzo*, middle. A place between, sometimes used to describe musical numbers between the acts of a play or a dish or drink to cleanse the palate in a meal. (I remember my grandmother using lime sherbert as an intermezzo.) The journey of a lifetime requires stopping places along the way, intermezzo oases for breathing and inviting the Inner Teacher to speak. In this field guide, poems provide those.

Listening, deep listening: The theologian Paul Tillich said the first duty of love is to listen. A kindergartener named Alec carefully explained to me that the words **listen** and **silent** have the same letters – just in a different order – and you can't do one without the other. Both listening and silence are essential as we move into the role of Elder, and that is where deep listening comes in. Deep listening requires the listener to be fully present, with no necessity to respond or to fix. The purpose is to create the space for the speaker to hear his or her own inner truth. Deep listening may include open, honest questions, which are explained below. A result of deep listening is often feeling heard into speech, as explained above.

Mobius, Mobius strip, Mobius journey: The Mobius strip illustrates the seamlessness of the inner and outer movement of the journey of becoming an Elder, of making our hidden wholeness visible. The dictionary tells us that the Mobius strip, named for the German mathematician A. F. Mobius, is a one-sided surface made by joining the ends of a rectangle after twisting one end through 180 degrees. Parker Palmer talks about the stages of growing into who we are, of developing our birthright gifts, as growing towards "life on the Mobius strip," a seamless flow of our inner life and outer world.

Questions; open, honest questions: We have found that questions offer us a much more fertile ground for this journey to wholeness than do answers. The words that Rainer Maria Rilke wrote to a young poet in 1903 still serve as important touchstones for us: "*...have patience with everything unresolved in your heart and try to love the questions themselves as if they were locked rooms or books written in a very foreign language. Don't search for the answers, which could not be given to you now because you would not be able to live them. And, the point is to live everything. Live the questions now. Perhaps then, someday far in the future, you will gradually, without even noticing it, live your way into the answer.*" Parker Palmer defines honest, open questions in *A Hidden Wholeness*: An honest question is one to which the asker cannot possibly know the answer. An open question is one that expands rather than restricts your area of exploration, one that does not push or even nudge towards a particular way of seeing or responding.

Paradox: The ability to understand paradox, to hold two seemingly opposite truths, to embrace both/and rather than either/or, is another important element of the journey toward becoming an Elder. As the scientist Niels Bohr said, "The opposite of a correct statement is a false statement. But the opposite of a profound truth may well be another profound truth."

Soft eyes: The idea of soft eyes often feels countercultural in a world that emphasizes sharp focus and is important in the journey toward becoming an Elder. We need to see each other with soft eyes, but even more, to see themselves that way. Author Sally Z. Hare often explains soft eyes by sharing a story from her Kellogg fellowship in Bali: "When I asked the Balinese elder who was my mentor while I was there to help me understand the Balinese childrearing practices that result in gentle, compassionate young people, she explained to me that they saw their children with soft eyes. The Balinese consider their children holy. The younger a person is, the closer her soul to heaven and the purer her spirit. Babies have just come from God, so they are not permitted to touch the impure earth before their first birthday and are carried everywhere. Balinese children are never left alone, nor are they ever physically punished, and rarely are they upset. So, this wise woman told me, we see them with soft eyes, like you would see someone you love... It's not that you don't see the imperfections; you just don't see their sharp edges."

Soul; connecting Soul and Role: "Nobody knows what the soul is," poet Mary Oliver writes in *Maybe*: "it comes and goes/ like the wind over the water." The soul has many names (Thomas Merton calls it true self; the Buddhists, original nature; Quakers, the inner light; Hasidic Jews, the spark of the divine; humanists, identity and integrity)– and Parker writes in *A Hidden Wholeness* that it doesn't matter *what* we name it, but *that* we name it matters a great deal. The soul is shy, making the creation of safe space very important if we are going to have a chance to hear that inner voice. Connecting soul (the inner) and role (how we show up in the outer world), the work of becoming an Elder, allows us to live with Integrity between the inner and the outer.

Thin place: In Celtic spirituality, thin places are where heaven and earth seem to touch. Thin place describes the field to which this field guide leads; that place in which we have the best chance of connecting soul and role as Elder, of seeing our hidden wholeness. In a thin place, we experience our connectedness to everything around us.

Ubuntu: This Nguni Bantu word literally means human-ness and is often translated as "humanity towards others." Since Nelson Mandela's presidency in South Africa, the term has spread from that region to other places, often through the writing of Desmond Tutu, who uses it to express the philosophical belief that we are all connected. On our journey to becoming an Elder, we embrace the paradox that the inner journey can only be undertaken by an individual, and yet it is too hard to take alone. Tutu's writing on Ubuntu offers language for this seemingly countercultural concept, another way to name the idea of solitude in community.

Undivided Life: Living a life of wholeness, of integrity, in which the Inner Self (soul) is congruent with the ways One shows up in the outer world (role).

Gratitudes

Writing is a paradox. Only I can write my own story – and I couldn't possibly do so without my community. I have learned it takes a village – and I am grateful you are in mine.

Megan LeBoutillier, thank you for friendship and companionship and encouragement – and especially for your willingness to be my editor. I could not have moved through that portal from writing for my own Reader Self to going public without you.

Susan Hitt, your skill as an editor and your love as my sister, combined in mystical ways as you offered your unique eye to my work.

Caroline Fairless, you have been a true cheerleader, creating a space in which I could both hear criticism and see the cracks where the Light gets in. That is nothing short of a miracle.

My Courage to Write Sisters, Veta and Jean and Haqiqa and Jonetta and Caroline, words are inadequate to describe my gratitude for your encouragement every Monday and your companionship in writing, as well as your deep listening and your help every time I was stuck. Your gentle honesty is what I wish every writer could have. I thank each and all of you again for your words in the Preface.

Linda Guris, as a friend and a Soul Sister and a

lifelong kindergarten teacher and a Courage to Teach pioneer, your commitment as early Reader was invaluable. You touched me deeply with your loving honesty – and inspired me to keep going.

Elaine Sullivan, your wisdom and grit and humor and kindness are such a gift. I treasure our friendship and am so grateful for your role in my life as Elder and Teacher.

Martha Timberlake, you dared invite me to add The ElderGarten to the Center for Renewal and Wholeness Facilitator Institute, even before you really knew what it was! Your trust deepened my belief in my Self.

Parker Palmer, your fingerprints are all over this book and all over my heart and soul.

Anne Swanson, I thank you for creating the space for me to meet Parker Palmer – and for your life-changing friendship. You inspire me and you make me laugh – and that, my Friend, is a rare combination.

Sandie Merriam, I am constantly grateful for your courage and your friendship and your standing with me in the Tragic Gap.

Jane Zalkin, your beautiful art has literally kept me moving forward with this book for more than a year. You created the cover as you listened to what I hoped to write, and then I wanted to write a book worthy of your cover. Your kindergarten teacher heart and your presence in my very first Courage to Teach are such a huge part of my whole journey.

Jean Richardson and Pat Mulroy, your belief in me has never wavered. Your work to register the name, your love, your gifts, your granola have nurtured me in every step of the journey.

Jim R. Rogers, my husband and partner and creative editor and the wife I have always wanted, there are no adequate words to express my gratitude for your always being there. I love you more. This book, like our life, is truly a co-creation of our Love.

And loving gratitude to Hope, who came at just the right time.

Sally

Dr. Sally Z. Hare, distinguished Singleton Professor
Emerita and founding director of the Center for
Education and Community at Coastal Carolina
University, is president of still learning, inc. She is a
product of South Carolina public education, from first
grade through her doctorate. As Dean of Graduate
and Continuing Education at Coastal Carolina for
a dozen years, she served in the role of teacher and
advisor and mentor and coach for more than 1,000
students. She served on the Kirkridge Retreat
and Study Center Board of Trustees for five years,
including four years as board chair. After a Kellogg
Fellowship changed her life in the early '90's, she
created the Kirkridge Courage Fellowship and the
ElderGarten Fellowship with the hope of changing
the lives of others.

Sally is a lifelong teacher and learner. Her passion is
reading – and she lives at the intersection of education
and community. Her Kellogg Fellowship took her
deeply into exploring community across cultures
and meeting Parker J. Palmer. After more than 30
years of working with Dr. Palmer in the Courage to
Teach and the Courage to Lead and the Center for
Courage & Renewal and the Center for Renewal and
Wholeness, Sally has co-created still learning, inc,

with her husband and partner, parenting and family life educator Jim Rogers. They live in Surfside Beach, SC, with Hope, their rescued supermutt. and many fairies and gnomes in their Fairy Forest.

Sally was named Phenomenal Woman in South Carolina, and Maya Angelou read the poem to her as she received the award. She was the editor and storycatcher for *The Story Mandala: Finding Wholeness in a Divided World*, as well as *Thin Places: Seeking the Courage to Live in a Divided World* and *Let the Beauty We Love Be What We Do: Stories of Living Divided No More*. She also authored a children's book, *Lucas and the Terribly-Trying Trying-Terribly Test* and a few poems and a number of other essays and articles, including *The Lehrergarten: A Vision for Teacher Education* in Living the Questions: Essays Inspired by the Work and Life of Parker J. Palmer (Intrator, Jossey Bass, 2005). *The Dance of a Lifetime: The Transaction of Individual and Community and Work* in Wintering into Wisdom (Kennesaw University Press, 2007); and *We Teach Who We Are: The Intersection of Teacher Formation and Educator Dispositions* in Dispositions in Teacher Education (Information Age Publishing, Volume 7 in Advances in Teacher Education, 2007).

Printed in the USA
CPSIA information can be obtained
at www.ICGtesting.com
LVHW091018231223
767295LV00046B/802